Ground, Wind, This Body

MARY BURRITT CHRISTIANSEN POETRY SERIES

Hilda Raz, Series Editor

The Mary Burritt Christiansen Poetry Series publishes two to four books a year that engage and give voice to the realities of living, working, and experiencing the West and the Border as places and as metaphors. The purpose of the series is to expand access to, and the audience for, quality poetry, both single volumes and anthologies, that can be used for general reading as well as in classrooms.

Mary Burritt
Christiansen
Poetry Series

Also available in the Mary Burritt Christiansen Poetry Series:

MEAN/TIME: Poems by Grace Bauer

América invertida: An Anthology of Emerging Uruguayan Poets edited by Jesse Lee Kercheval

Untrussed: Poems by Christine Stewart-Nuñez

Family Resemblances: Poems by Carrie Shipers

The Woman Who Married a Bear: Poems by Tiffany Midge

Self-Portrait with Spurs and Sulfur: Poems by Casey Thayer

Crossing Over: Poems by Priscilla Long

Heresies: Poems by Orlando Ricardo Menes

Report to the Department of the Interior: Poems by Diane Glancy

The Arranged Marriage: Poems by Jehanne Dubrow

For additional titles in the Mary Burritt Christiansen Poetry Series, please visit unmpress.com.

Ground, Wind, This Body poems

TINA CARLSON

UNIVERSITY OF NEW MEXICO PRESS | ALBUQUERQUE

Library of Congress Cataloging-in-Publication Data
Names: Carlson, Tina, 1953– author.
Title: Ground, wind, this body : poems / Tina Carlson.
Description: First edition. | Albuquerque : University of New Mexico Press, 2017. |
Series: Mary Burritt Christiansen Poetry Series
Identifiers: LCCN 2016013139 (print) | LCCN 2016024404 (ebook) |
ISBN 9780826357793 (pbk. : alk. paper) | ISBN 9780826357809 (electronic)
Classification: LCC PS3603.A75332 A6 2017 (print) | LCC PS3603.A75332
(ebook) | DDC 811/.6—dc23
LC record available at https://lccn.loc.gov/2016013139

Cover photograph by Diana Hooper Bloomfield. Author photograph by Mia Carlson.
Designed by Catherine Leonardo
Composed in Dante MT Std 11.5/13.5

for Mia

Only because it's violent to the core
The world grows gardens

—*Clive James*

Contents

Gloss and Silt

War Is a Cradle

Light-Years

I claim a granite outcrop on the day we visit our mountain homesite.
The dirt is thick with flint and the air smells of sap.
The happy family eats sandwiches on a cliff,
makes plans to build under a luminous canopy of pines.
Below, plains steam in the afternoon heat.
Light-years away from our daily lives, we draw rooms on the ground.
Columbines in the kitchen, cool moss for a rug.
Covered in sap and grit, my brothers wrestle for space below in a
    gully.
My father sketches ideas on a pad. *They are selling land cheap*, he
    claims.
He found this plot on the canyon's steep edge.
We feed our meat sandwiches to the squawking jays and bold
    squirrels.
My mother watches the sun set.
My father, a wild and rough architect, designs our future until it gets
    dark.

War Is a Cradle

Silence is born in a war high above an Italian village, in snow, on skis, hiding from the Germans. Because in some recent time your people were German too, you are not sure whom to kill. You find the enemy freezing to death in a cave, some months older than your seventeen years, eyes the same blue as the ice that melts on your boots.

War is wild and makes you forget the taste of meringue on your mother's fingers after baking, or the warm brick of your home in summer.

You shoot him in the head and hold him afterward, his blood pooling in your lap. You keep his gun as a souvenir. You begin to hear his sisters singing in your head, and the branches you break sound like bones.

In the small makeshift hospital, they bathe you in cream because you have forgotten how to speak and cannot tell them your name.

She nearly drowns in a lake near a pink hotel. Because the boat has overturned, no one is listening. The water is clear and barely shattered by her flailing. They pull her out, half-dead in her party dress, which leaves ripples in its flouncy wake. She marries the one ravaged by war when his skin was still soft. She will fear water until she grows old and tired of drowning, and will teach herself to swim. Together they will crack open their children's heads on the stairs, like bright new eggs.

The Core

Once they were young and laughing. Imagine
what life can offer up, if split open like her body

with his hand on her thin back or lit by her smile against the lost
    hope of an afternoon.
Look how they shut out the rest of the day, adorned as it may be

in liquid light, mountain breath, wind. Everything seems possible
with the war just over and the bowl of plastic fruit on his mother's
    table

still gleaming: each piece perfect
and untouched, seedless to the core.

Ski Lesson

Bend your knees, he warns me.
My father slaloms around trees
and signposts but after each tenuous turn
I fall. He is patient, joyful. His face is grizzled
with cold. He skied the Alps in war. I want to be home
on warm cork floors. I take off my gloves and suck on my frozen
    fingers.
He speeds off, the wool of his ski pants flapping behind his knees.
I bend my legs, make grooves in the soft powder with my wooden
    army skis.
Follow the tracks my father makes.

The House My Father Built

Here are the rooms
possible after snow,
musky with the smells of boys.

Baked bread, steaming walls.
A blue refrigerator. Heat
under cork floors, cool curtained spaces.

Black eye of a pond, fire.
Brother burns a scar on his leg
in the shape of a trout.

Earaches. Ice dripping in the garden,
glass blown in on itself. Every weather,
loving the green and the absence of green.

Meat sandwiches, hats of wet wool.
This is my history,
its rooms and blood.

Girls with War in Our Blood

The field is dry
and hard as bone.
We dig, dig below to the marrow
where worms burrow in wet grit
and memory sleeps between sod and iron,
death's deep and dark aquarium.

⌐

Girls with war in our blood.
Trees stand watch over our daily expeditions,
smell the musk of men waiting to die or kill
still pungent in our fathers,

salute the sky
call, *mother,*
mother, give me
storms
that rend
and cleanse

⌐

We dance near pond's edge
in the starry nights

find our ways out of windows
through wet grass.

An invisible chorus of toads sings
to the moon that floats across the silk water.

⌐

Unzip
my skin
and the gun
in my heart
blows the world
to bits in
a flash

My family
watches me
writhe
on the floor
rage-wedged
between
a wail and
the ground

War's molt sounds animal

⌒

Horses stomp and feed.
We lure them with apples
across the fenced field.
One bites a rose
on my chest,
looking for grain.

⌒

Every ditch sings for summer.
Water gliders swim
in the shoes I hide
on my way to school.
Swallows scallop the sky
above iris farms and pondgrass.

⌒

We lie in the arms of
cottonwood trees,
sleep in their broad
branches, steer the ships
of their heft toward
the horizon.

⸝

The other fathers watch
as mine chases
my brothers across the field.
He was never the same
after the war,
they tell their daughters.
My father is blind for blood
in those boys still new.

⸝

There is a death that lives.
In our dreams owls cover every surface.
Apples, woodpiles, streetlamps.
Owls alive in fields
gritty with the mud
of our repentances.

The Burial

My father buries the bird
in a bland field: a crow still glossy
with its memory of flight
and release. How he finds himself there in that brief
digging, fingering the dirt
of his children's field, the small nest he
quarries there,
how gently he lays that
blackbird down as if it is the heart
he once carried in his own boy's chest
before the war
and shock of his life
shot him down and placed him here,
burying what used to fly
in the fall weeds
and grave of ground.

Our Lives Aloft

My brothers cook up an idea to live on the trampoline.
They pole-vault across the yard and jump from room to room in their
    bouncing home.
Beds made of gunnysacks.
Dry cereal to eat.
We jump and twirl and even flip through the day, our lives aloft.
In the borders of night, our eyes are ponds.
Everything is moisture and glistens.
Some flowers open then, waiting for moths.
We sleep outside in the dark, as crickets nod us to sleep.
We dream our parents come to watch and sit, hand in hand, celebrate
    the sheltering trees and their children, lifted up and laughing.

Early-Morning Meditation

Our mother sits by the stove,
sipping her tea and making crumbs
of dry toast. In these moments,
the orange-painted horse on the sill
looks out over the long pastured
land. She sees the others nipping
at their oats, pawing the ground.
The children have been silenced.
The world wakes up under a spool of light.

Instead of Light

Sin

The mouth is given,
the sky and its snowy
silences, night's wet
breath.

What is the horizon,
a five-year-old's hips
and her fists, opened?

The priest bends down,
donut dust on his cassock.
He wants to touch her hair,
wants to sweeten her
between his teeth.

The red pump, with its fisted
blood. Here sin is a song,
a field of heat, a tether.

She immigrates to the land
of absence. Dreams of capture:
her own voice greening
behind the glass.

A Span of Storm

Snow glints: a bright
nerve of light
against the glass.
Ice drips
as the sun
conspires
to turn this day
to mud.

I sigh a single song.
I am six years old
and my hands
smell of smoke.

Time
threads a span
of storm
and melt. I lie
on the warm cork
floor, lapping up
the books
like milk.

Instead of Light

1.
The night is fat with cold and cloud,
the den a holy cave, gleaming
teeth and eyes, a hungry place,
a mouth. I arrive with my father
in my yellow pajamas. It is one a.m.
though my father's eyes shine
blue like a dome of morning
sky. I was dreaming of birds
falling from a sky of milk—

The pornographer prays to the gods of stupor
and submission. Loves to open what has never
been opened, turned on by the camera's endless click,
the sacred theft. Our child bodies lie on little
green tables with the metal taste
of a gun in our mouths. The small meat of our bodies
shared by the pack of parents and assistants—

I watch through a grimy window
the mirrored light of the moon, believe
a lamp. It shines back at me, across
the broad diameter of night where I am
the pain of not-enough-air.
TV commercials blare in the next room, the heater clicks.
The moistened mouth of a woman tells me I am nothing,
silence is my only currency. She is a bear
standing over my small perch where I learn
to unstitch myself from the harrow of bone and skin.
This becomes a definition of home: the infinite mouth of night,
air made of feathers.

Outside, snow falls quiet as a moth.
Settles over the town its cold white gift
of cover-up. My father pockets the money
he gains, spent by morning on milk and bread.

2.
Tiny rivers of blood in my ears
a pulsing tide, icy feet, mind made
of song and the sugary taste of words.
Like *pale, crisp, luminous.* Blood is a rose
on the morning snow. I shine an orange light
over the syllables, then play
with their shadows on the walls.
Glint, curve, ashen.
Hunger becomes soup, cold a warm bath.
The grime of my father's hands, a milky solace.
I stand behind the innocent child he wanted to be.
Limbic, shorn, silent.

3.

Each night I die there again
on the little green table, fear the beds whose skins
I peel back to rest, the predatory breath
of night. Trees shudder their dry leaves
in a breeze. I dream the moon is a wide lit face,
floats to the ground and waits outside
our home. A man who loves plants opens the door
of her mouth and gathers up the child you were,
years ago, places you in my arms
like a bouquet.

4.

You too knew the teeth of that place.
You become a running star, the fastest legs
in town. You will race from your home to mine
and we will hide in a cave of tree branches,
sugar our mouths with licorice and the
green stalks of weeds. Speed is your balm,
you are mine, my first love, my mirror.
We never speak of the captive nights but fill
ourselves with sweets in the day's free heat.
When you are grown, ready for your final
escape, you will remember the gun, harbor it
in your college dorm room for weeks. They will find you fetal,
wrapped around its unexploded body like a cocoon.
An empty bottle of pills under your last pillow.
No note, but I understand your message,
Only I can write that gun out of my own mad mouth.

5.
I love to lie on the ground
for her ballast of living green and holiness of dirt.
A valence of quiet, the undertow of magma
pulsing through. Her body is the dense memory of our histories.
Every moon of thought, every motion of kindness
and cruelty, transmuted.
I am buoyant lying there, on her whirling
heft, her lap a curve and horizon. Sum of loam
and fracture, we breathe in unison on cracked ground,
sea bottoms. I am a canyon cut deep, a list of fault lines.
She tames me with her touch.

Perimeter of War

Our home eventually blew down,
stained planks shattered
under the winds of his panic.
We held our jackets high

over our heads like bright sails
and tried to fly away. He lived
in the propane fumes of his van,
trash collecting under

its axled belly. Each day he called out
to his enemies, hunkered behind
the unkempt hedges. Yellow flowers
dared to bloom on those greening branches

at the perimeter of war, our homeless home.
Our small bodies airborne for only moments:
sewn as we were to that darkening battlefield
of our father's mind.

Inmates

1.

I used to dream of incarcerations. Captives
straining to remember the sugary moon.
Yearning for a breeze,
ghosts tapping at the glass.

I would wake a girl again, breathing hard,
covered in blue blankets, momentarily free.
Picturing snow up to my knees,
bird bones in the shallow bowl of a ditch.

2.

A drive to Denver in the sixties
was a stretch of wind over farm fields.
To cousins, roller coaster parks, an uncle smelling of gin.
My brothers and I feigned sleep on the cigarette-fumed seats of the
    car
on the way home. Towns in the distance
were yellow beads in the shadowed lap
of mountains.

My father drove the old Valiant across
pastures and plains, now buried in malls and glassy
offices. We whispered our own languages
in the back seat.

Outside, a huge night pushed in against
the window glass: we pressed our faces,
peered out.

Shapeshifters

The pornographer washes
us with light.

We are small stones
bundled in sockets of bone.

Hard as stone,
soft as bundles, bone-fed.

Hardened to stone,
softened into marrow,

we are bundled
onto the bony platform.

He sells this feast to the hungry:
he is the table, we are the meat.

The Blue Pool

My brother remembers
my father driving the whole family
to "my boyfriend" the pornographer's
apartment, then speeding off
to get root beer floats.

I stayed behind next to the small blue pool,
held still by the man's dark hands. My mother
remembers the wild gleam in the eye
of the fancy man who took me in
and turned me into something else.

She remembers the raw red
of his convertible and the glitz
of his cameras, his black
slicked hair. My brother wondered
what was so funny about
a man five times my age
being my boyfriend,
and why I would be left behind,
a small girl watching the car drive away?

We never spoke of these things until
I learned to reenter the secret cave
of my body, to breathe myself back
into my own pod of skin
and pulsing rivers of memory.

My father doesn't remember the harm
or heat of those days.
I remember his pale feet,
simple and girl-like with garden grit
in the nails. How he loved to walk in the mud
without shoes. How he loved to paint my face
with dirt. How I thrilled to be twirled in the air
until my small world started to turn
on its axis. I remember

distilling myself down
in the pornographer's den,
into the piney woods
outside, the
cement sidewalk,
the table I lay on.
Dense and numb,
then lifting out
of my body
over the tops
of the homes of
happy families sitting
down to dinner,
waving at my family
as they drove by
to pick me up again.

The day my daughter is five, my father calls after years. *Send me her photograph*, he says. As if the years have unspooled on film in his mind, as if the children line up to be taken. I feel the pulse in me turn to current. I understand the protesting students, standing their ground in front of military shooters. Women, refusing to leave their homes in a storm. Children, lighting fires in a field to warn the others. His headlights shine through the wire. My daughter laughs, just then, out back on the swing. *Good-bye*, I say, and mean it.

Summer Nights

After rain, the earth shines in gratitude. We are nine,
awake on wet grass and the sky, a vast black cup of stars.
Because our lives are small fires buried under dry fields,
the muddy homes of childhood, auditoriums of weeds, and trees.
Even discomfort glistens here.
The whole world breathes together, watches messages
pass across the wide face of the moon. We were born into wildness
after the war. Each year, watch the hillsides burn aspen yellow,
then the wind changes everything to brown.
For you, I am an arsonist.
Our fathers take aim at us behind doors with imaginary weapons,
still living in battle. Almost criminal, our desire to thrive in this
   world.
Our futures arrested, like the cat's gift in the doorway:
birdlike, perfectly curled into the shape of an egg, gelatinous.

Hometown Astronaut, 1962

Ready for anything in his slick silver suit
smiling out from a bubble hood. Our world sat still
while he fired up the engine, air exploding beneath him.
On the ground, my body pressed into the comfort of dirt
with just the red brick of the school nearby, boys shouting down the
    block.
Insides dense as wood, then flying out over the field. Hours twirled
    by.
The earth was silty, sweet with the warm smell of spring,
fresh horse manure, new buds blushing on the trees.
Every day was a new kind of wilderness.
Small bags of sweets a numbing pleasure. The noise of boys shooting
pop bottle rockets and a man still screaming out the war.
Weapons of every kind came in handy. A slingshot of hair ties
shot a marble into the pack of boys. One cried so hard he turned blue.
Everything stopped for a few minutes.
TV told us, *reach for the stars. The sky's the limit.*
We looked up to space like our hero, envied his fame and defiance of
    gravity.
Even the astronaut's tears floated in space, like tiny crystals in the
    emptiness.
Imagine the view, circling round the small earth from that distance.
Everything into focus then: floating like a feather,
as far away from home as you could get.

Occupied Territories

Each Small Heaven

Air
The wind is god, exhaling.
Holds up her red coat and she is airborne, unhinged
from gravity, from her body's watery weight, full of sleep,
into the deep cool breath of the mountain.

Too little breath for the mother who opens her mouth and wheezes
    into the night.
Eats dry toast on a turquoise plastic plate, eyes wide open
and afraid as the children bring stick nests
with small fragments of eggs, pink quartz, dandelion bouquets.

Children breathe for the ones they count on,
gasping on flowered sheets. The father's madness a bitter smell,
like blood, rusted metal, the aftershock of lightning in a summer
    storm.

Earth
Everything, broken. The mother's bones too thin and cracking open,
father's mind mashed by war and worry, fracture of wood stained
    brown
and baking in the sun, the home he built by hand. Window glass
    pocked
by stones and misguided bird flight.

Too many children who wield sticks with nails fighting the ghosts of
    ancestors.
He offers his daughter the worm and she takes it because she is used
    to his offerings—
body parts, black licorice, sorrow, taking in and becoming him. The
    worm
is cool and salty, full of grit. She chews slowly and swallows.

The mother tends the round, bulbed garden, print of tulips on her
     summer blouse.
Hears a piece of heaven pass by in clouds threatening rain.

Fire
The girl lights her brother on fire, his tiny leg a deep, orange flame.
Screams bring the others out of hiding. His small hip open for the
     grafting.
The children love to play with fire. Lit sticks, incinerator smoke in
     yellow fields
full of cottonwoods, horse sweat. The heated stone of childhood in a
     father's wild,
blue eyes. The mother prays for rain in a cool back room.

Yellow light behind glass in an airless cave of home, a cigarette left
     burning in a tray.
The girl drinks red Kool-Aid out of a blue metal cup under the star's
     vast glittering.
Later, she will be drawn to the smoldering mouths of volcanoes, the
     cool smoke
of evenings settling in.

Water
More children arrive from their watery worlds and the mother grows
haggard. Drowning for air, she learns to swim in a small garden pool.
Each year, the father believes he is dying. He holds the new heads of
his sons in his hands like soft rounds of fruit which he will later split
open on the sides of a groaning piano. He prunes each green hedge
with long rusting shears, waits for the moment of dark breathlessness.
The girl wakes up from a night of his breath in her ear. Each small
heaven so full of risk: the bright-yellow faces of flowers, nests of red
birds, gleaming eyes of new boys, the season's subtle shifting, gray
strands of rain on the horizon.

The Hunt

My father lies in a clean bed, dreaming in sheets the color
of sky. The wind is a thin child's call, the broad
back of his mother turning away. He doesn't recognize
his sagging uniform of skin or the perilous
ocean of his room where strangers
call his name. Each sound is a startle.

He would like to let go. Dreams bring him back:
a young boy at the table,
waiting for his mother to turn around
and feed his heart
before war became his father.

Across the ocean, muscled and sleek,
a pod of dolphins swims into a cove,
lured by hunger and the chaos of nets and noise.
What my father's life must seem:
the heart's coved capture,
the killings that inevitably follow.

Occupied Territories

1.
My ancestors take their books,
paste each printed page onto another,
until the words call out, the breath,
the blood of a book.

Then they cut a hole in the middle
for treasure. By the time we arrive
the holes are empty,
words bleeding out.

My drowning mother tries
to learn to swim. In water she
sings "God Bless America"
in secret code.

Loneliness and the baby learn
early to be friends. I have
turned love outward to the mangled
men in the street.

China calls the horizon back
into the room of my daughter.

I dream the child I was.
Find me, she calls,
I am a treasure, buried alive.

2.

Smothered birds and wild horses migrate
across these occupied territories.

I enter a room pale as a moon in winter.
There you are, smiling across tables and chairs

scrubbed clean back to the trees
where they were born.

I remember to say good-bye,
know this is a dream

and that you have died
as the windows look out

on the snaking canals
and wild crags of mountains

and I am standing everywhere
I have ever lived at once

in the spare white room of death
while a pine forest whispers

outside a small door flowered
with paper from the cabin where

I was born as my life
circles back from here

to you, smiling across
a moon of a room

lit from each moment we have lived
and the invitation of what is to follow.

I Wish You Were Here

The river is a woman singing of heartbreak
surrounded by birds and smooth
pockets of stone. I wish you were here
instead of blowing across the dry field
as dust. In the sleek fur of my dreams
you rustle up stories about
children who live in the sun.
I love everything
I remember and don't remember
about you. In the wood of your chairs
live savannahs we might
have seen, full of animal scents
and the lovely emptiness of years
between my life now
and your hands, pointing the way.

Midnight

Bees float in a sea
of black irises.

A man lies in water
and I hold his head above the waves.

My brothers stand in the shallows.
Our mother steps out of the story and disappears.

Home is a cool breeze
under threat of a storm.

We inhabit the little metal rooms.
In one version, we escape

through a drain
in the prison sink.

The world of the open sky
boasts of happiness.

My brothers are thin
and high pitched in their cries.

There has been an accident.
I swim across a dry pool

to mountains
without a map.

The Medicine Woman Speaks of Suicide

Remove her ring
from your home,
bury it in the mountains.
Find the storm and look up
into the falling flakes,
tell her,
go on into the wind
without me.
Yell so loudly
granite understands
your meaning.
Tell her it will be okay.
Tell her you will be okay
without her.
Tell her light, the light,
pray light
will take her away.

Wild Wind

Your daughters are angry you've found another love
so soon after the last one, and the one before:
you weave a wreath of women to hang
on your heart. How you turn from the door when
your daughters come knocking.

I could say your yearning is a tropical bird
lost in a winter storm. Or a white horse starving
in the neighbor's field.
Your daughters carry pain in their own hearts now.
They stand at the door calling.

I want to show them one day of your life as a child:
Our father's hands on your ankles, your shaved head
bouncing up the outdoor stairs, the crush of stone
reddening your scalp.
How the cork floor kissed and held you after.

They would see you listen at the ground
for snow, the blue sky of your eyes
clouding over. Our mother hovered near,
warming at the stove. Your bony boy's trust
broken glass at her feet.

Each new love cradles your head in her lap
as you bloom in the temporary thaw
of a woman's touch, the windows
curtained and closed, the wild wind of our father
at bay.

Let the World See

He lay on the floor for five days.
It was the same floor he lay on
as a boy dreaming of slick mountain backs
of snow, and the sweet blue body of the sister
who died before he was born, the girl
he was supposed to be.

His mother closed in on herself
when she saw the small blue fish
that was her daughter.
She taught the sons that followed
to hate the marrow that made
their blood.

He killed when he was still a child.
He killed and carried the young soldier
on his back for the rest of his life until he couldn't,
until he became too old to carry anyone
and he fell, face down on the floor for five days
with the soldier and the sister who couldn't grow up.
Their lost lives swam in his spine,
thinned his blood, kept the tears from coming out.

Until his son. The dirty window opened up and let some air in.
Let the son see,
let the world see what has happened.

On the coracle of floor, he was just who he was.
Not the disappointing son, the killer, the child molester,
the hedge cutter, the wife beater, the dirty unshaven
disappointment of a father, the propane-loving, fast-walking,
snaggletoothed man.
The floorboards held him like a child
and now his eighty-eight-year-old body that smelled of soot and
grime.

There was a time when the mountains
were blanketed with snow and there was no war.
He remembers the slick descent and the rising up again.
Children in parkas the color of sucking candy,
all lined up, watching him glide, his singing flight.

He is thankful for the peace that comes
with no water for days, the slide into doze
into half-lived memory. He dreams of the boy
he shot, and sees him lying on the floor.
I'm sorry, he tells him, *it was war and we were boys.
Sometimes I think you were the lucky one after all.*
The German soldier smiles,
his mouth a stain that moves across his face
until it becomes the floor again and melts.

He cradles his sister who died before him,
her skin the color of thin milk. *I'm sorry*,
he says, *for taking your place. It was death
and then birth, I couldn't undo.*
She becomes the bird outside his window singing.

His life could end this way, but it doesn't.
The son brings others, carrying stretchers
and bags of fluid, who listen to his heart, barely beating.
He wakes in a bed where he is shaven
and bathed clean with lemon-smelling soap.
The years wash off, and he is a boy,
no longer wishing he was the girl, or the soldier,
the ones who died so he could live, the ones
he has carried until the past pushed him over.
He is alone in a bed; he is blanketed and fed.

Still Missing

This morning I smell fall. A cool
and dense warning breeze
close in the park's dark elms.
The hawk's early call: sharper,
urgent. I think of my brothers as boys
clad in camouflage jammies,
wielding sticks and my father's old,
dead gun. Fall meant a wild wind,
not like the summer, captured in green.
Kitchen beatings, the smell of wool
and leather in my mother's blue closet.
If only I could reach back
through history's hall of seasons
and shelter those small bald heads
and hearts from their daily
woundings. Into the fields
of their wars, pale with drying
grasses. How those boys, even now as men,
are still missing. Gazing down the darkening
street into the eyes of oncoming cars,
they hurl rocks from trees onto
the slick and endless traffic
that streams by without stopping.

Gloss and Silt

Ojo Caliente: Metamorphoses

1.
The summer was shattering.
Too much pressure and heat
change the nature of stone.
For this, we walk a dry path
under the spiraling flight of two eagles
disappearing into blue.

2.
The lightness of letting go is good to sink into.
Golden and afloat, leaves drift, sonorous
in their descent. We pass ancient villages,
small mounds along the stony path. Peaks
blue in the distance shimmer under snow.

3.
Along the trail, we look for snakes
in cool cracks of granite.
The magnitude of the day opens,
a way in. Mica gleams from dark caves,
flaked light, glass.

4.
Nothing lasts forever.
Even here, the gods of heat and water
break through red stone into steamy pools
of sulfur, arsenic, iron.

5.
A woman with cats on her socks wanders
across a bluff. Bodies are sanctuaries
of loneliness. We remember to look up,
find the fingernail of a moon.

What Is Buried Turns to Gloss and Silt

The more broken I become, the more
I find my way. Where are you,
now that I want to know? The blue
bedspread. Light and stained
wood. Myself as a girl.

My own hands
in my mouth,
fingernails bit
to the quick.

If only the bridge
of my ribs could
span the field
and all that is buried there.

The young hustle out of that place.
In time, the air is alive with pings and trills.
Riffing and shredding,
weeds sing in the wind.
The path I follow smells of pine.

You, Lover of Hills

Bones pale and smooth
as sleet. Hold my hand, you lover
of hills. Bent against stone that crumbles,
roots pull out with our touch.

The baby has grown her teeth. Thimbles
and thread make a path to the door. How
tenuously we are sewn to this ground.
Fruit in small packages. The world
with its sloped edge.

After you die, you are a young, pale
girl, thin hand cool in mine. *I am
vigorous now*, you say.

On Not Drowning

1.
The hospital room pulses
with tubes and pumped air
where she lies in her bed,
propped up and central,
the queen you have
always known her to be.
It is obvious
the medical team on her case
has given up because
they keep their eyes covered
and watch a storm forming on the horizon.
Look how they miss her bony arms
waving wide circles:
she is dancing with death, you imagine,
showing her stuff. You hum tunes for her.
You think if they would just loosen
the tubing and sheets
she might fly right out of that bed,
leave behind a tangled cape of blankets
and petals of blood.

2.

She swims and the water is cold—
a child on the shore
and forests swarmed by bees—
she treads through the bleed in her brain,
keeps afloat after vessels give out,
toward a girl, calling,
or is it a bird,
winging messages about dying,
the waves she will have to pass through,
to land where leaves rain from trees
and orange birds fill the sky—
she has never wanted
to leave you stranded in this pale room—
makes strokes big and broad
toward the girl, whose name she cannot remember.

3.

When the complications of thought
and speech unravel in her mouth,
she tells you how her arms were calling
the sad room of waiting.
How death was watery,
its buoyancy uterine,
how she was a girl
standing on a bank with trees and bees.
Or was it birds and buzzing branches?
How she heard you sing
across her ruptured rivers
and swam back into that sacred
cave of the hospital room,
the temporary harbor of you.

Equinox

Under traffic, a sparrow clings lightly to blue tissue,
scooped for its nest in the poplar's bent, smooth body.

Wind pulses at the door all day. You cook meat
in a black kettle; its juices drool. My hungry body

left you in the dream of a blue motel. Empty-handed
you began to dance, sang a song for everybody.

When is a comet a simple blurred eye of dust
and ice? This woman lives in a blanket, is somebody.

She is always looking for home. Wind has helped,
and lovers. They appear in night's deep body

and love her with the memory of brown wood and snow
in spring. The only home we know: ground, wind, this body.

Mt. Taylor

The sign says Gooseberry Trail
and we follow through aspen
bare and thin as fine hair.
What we hope for is a mountain,
frozen across a chilled desert.
It is on grasses,
frayed and blown,
that we slow and sleep
for the first time in days.
My body is windy,
knotted with confusion.
Above, spruces huddle
blue as a bruise,
thick and silent.
We climb across the black slag of basalt,
snow clutched in its blisters.
Ravens laugh in huge flocks.
On the top, a rusted metal box
tethered by wire to a stone.
We pry open its thin messages
that wait like babies
to be held.
"God lives" and "I am dying
but I haven't told Eddie yet."
We scribble our prayers on blue paper—
"Bring back the rain" and "Let the war end soon"—
start down in the frayed, gray hours.
What we hope for remains hidden,
but so close, like winter,
we can smell it.

Mirage

The sky is the lightest blue with the thumbprint of a moon at the
    horizon.
We eat eggs doused in cheese next to the indoor shooting range.
Shots sound like thunder in the distance, or bowling balls hitting
    their mark.
A table of police officers jokes their way through breakfast, guns snug
    in their holsters. They are taught to kill, their mostly young faces
    laughing into their plates.
You taught me to taste dirt at each bend in the trail, how the grit and
    spice of it
changed close to water and under the owl's nest. You swallow a bullet
    of bread
and a breeze loosens up the day. Your wrists are pale as bone, smooth
    as the cream you pour without caution. Grasshoppers animate the
    synapses between tables.
You tell me there is an explosion of them from heat and drought. I
    want
to plant feathers in your hair. I want to clean the glob of cheese off
    your collar.
My heart is a tambourine you play in the moments that serve you.
You love the clean-eyed target, din of the range.
I crave the silence of your wrist in the palm of my hand.

Promises of God and Mud

In a wooden room a woman reads words of the ancients
and speaks of longing, the open flower of a soul

urging god to appear, and on the other side of glass
is the golden world: bunch grasses bent over in winter

wind, red- and orange-lit sandstone hills,
and she wonders, *what if god goes away?*

how do you stay awake when everything is falling?
stone glazed with a layer of frost, the sky a vast

blue arc full of invisible stars over the terrible state
of this world where innocence explodes in Baghdad, Mumbai,

and we pray for the sick as a flock of blackbirds dances over plains
so golden they gleam up into their own shimmering light, and the
    wind

smells of wet leaves and a hint of snow and we call out to the
    displaced
and hungry of the Congo, the small dazed boy separated from his
    family

in flight, honor our friend's new cancer, as water keeps flowing
under its thin skin of ice, and my daughter finds deer tracks

in sand on a bluff. So much beauty and injury
are possible: *stay awake*, the woman warns us, for the momentary

promises of god and mud,
steam rising off the pond's morning skin,
pulsing caves of the heart.

Mathematics of the Adopted Daughter

Each night is a breezy routine. I wash the purple
plastic bowls and air wisps over empty plates.
My daughter learns quadratic equations
where every x and y mate up and create order.
What is x when y is the loss of a country
divided by fish in the ponds of her birth?
Compute the value of lost parents pulsing
an ocean of night. Add the tension of glass,
each molecule held tight before the inevitable break.
When we met, she was wrapped in centuries of clothes,
the sum of all the heat and care of mothers before me.
We could hardly make our way through the buttery mornings.
When she was four, I threw a peach at her
all the sweetness orange on the blue-tiled floor.
Multiply these fingers by all the Chinese words
she never learned and the moon
is a plum you can split with your teeth.
Graph the green axis of rice near her birth,
count my arms holding her until she sleeps.

Small Girl and the Vastness

Lotus blossoms float white stars in the Chinese ponds.
The air is thick and pale. A man sells sweet potatoes,
orange meat cracked open over coal.

A truck passes full of young pigs headed toward slaughter.
Inside you, your mother swims in a green and steamy beginning.
At night flooded fields froth with rice.

Clouds breathe like dragons. Nine stands for power in this place
of lost girls and missing trees. Cormorants with wires around their
    necks
fish without swallowing for the fisherman floating on bamboo.

The river's banks rot with greens. Light on the water the color of
    blood, and gold.
Ponds fill with rain, women breathe in the hot sweet smell of the
    tobacco factory.
You were left along the road, bleak and bound in wool.

We lose our verbs and feast at round tables,
ducks roasted in plums. Birds sculpted out of carrots and dumplings
filled with nut paste and lemon.

Terra-cotta warriors are made of mud and guard the fear of death.
Vendors sell rounds of bread soaked in red chile oil, fish heads lined
    up on plates,
women who could be your mother stream past on bikes at shift's end.

Embryo of Light

for my daughter

1.

At night, you appear blurred as the edge of a cloud.
Like the moon's mouth, you bleed.
In a room full of white curtains and the smell of my grandmother
you grow animal in my arms. We breathe underwater, touching
    fingers.
I dream you dream me, blow through the night without waking.

2.

The moon is a late, red eye. Boneless as shadows,
trees secrete their list of sound. You will be born
between the dreamer and all that has been lost.
Each delicate darkness enfolds you,
small embryo of light.

3.

Wingless, I fly night's mouth: darkness exploding
with fire and prayer. Stars exhale light, clouds, cool and temporary.
Your birth mother holds up her dress: her huge belly is nothing to
    hide.
I wonder at the way animals gather around her. Everything she
    touches
comes back to life, even the bird dead for weeks.
Don't you see the fires? I ask your mother.
She licks her bowl clean as I stomp the blackened ground.
She tucks her unborn baby to sleep on a tray.
Explosives wrapped in white; none of us know what to do with such
    danger.
Birth begins loneliness the midwife tells us.

4.

Daughter, fly with me into this bowl of sky
that holds a stunned earth, purple with sleep. Hills
the color of bad teeth snake across its back.
Fire eats the ground.
You are infinite and awake.

5.

On an unmade bed, I pee circles around you. You seize
in my arms, lakes bloom on your back. The past sings
and floods. Your pregnant mother watches us from across the room
as I finger your wounds, rub raw egg on our bodies.
We will write music on the walls.

6.

Once, a round building. I search every direction
except the center, where you wait.
Fish grow in the places they tried to kill.
How delicate, the memory of breathing
before we are born.

7.

I prepare to go home across a breath of water.
Under rain, this city is all the cities I have ever lived in,
full of stands of art. I eat beaded flags for lunch.
I look for my mother, and she is there, a young woman
who does not yet know me, standing in a circle of women.
Look for blue, the vendor tells me, eat potatoes.

8.

Everything I reach for disappears.
Boats line the harbor, leave before we find our ticket.
Maps turn to air in my hands.
I sit on furniture on the trail and talk to strangers.
How will I ever find you? Temporary as blue in the evening.
As pines call to winter, I'll call to you.

9.
Each road is a river. Blackbirds line the banks,
dark as oil, preening. I carry my mother on my back,
swimming across her many histories.
The spell of generations weighs us into slow travelers.
We search the riddle of home, its bulbed gardens,
a cupped ring of earth. Instead, home is the watery smell
of lost mothers. Blue flowers lean from their cribs,
wind folds the trees into sadness. I feel you like an undertow:
dream's thick cord, the pulse of dark and wet between us.

Acknowledgments

The following poems have been previously published in various forms in the following journals:

The Best of Kore Press 2012: "Perimeter of War"
Blue Mesa Review: "Mt. Taylor"
bosque (the magazine): "Instead of Light," "Mirage," "Our Lives Aloft,"
    and "Promises of God and Mud"
New Mexico Mercury: "Ojo Caliente: Metamorphoses"

Thank you to everyone at the University of New Mexico Press.

Thank you to my mentors and teachers: Laurie Kutchins, Margaret Randall, Joy Harjo, Valerie Martinez, Lisa Gill, Hilda Raz, Lynn Miller

Thank you to Laurie Hause, Lynda Miller, Christina Squire, Jill Root, Kim Feldman, Jude Marx, Joy Jacobson, and Katherine DiBella Seluja for your friendship, writing support, inspiration, and ballast in the writing of this book

And to Mia, my muse

About the Author

Tina Carlson is originally from Boulder, Colorado, where she studied molecular biology and fell in love with the natural world. She has been writing poems since she was a nine-year-old girl scribbling notes in a small yellow notebook high in a cottonwood tree next to the vacant lot near her home. She currently lives in Albuquerque, New Mexico, and works as a psychiatric nurse practitioner. She has published poems in *Blue Mesa Review, American Journal of Nursing, Waving, Not Drowning, The Best of Kore Press 2012*, and *bosque (the magazine)*. Her poems work to uncover the confluences of paradox, the places where beauty and sacredness intersect with the underbelly of life.